Terrance Anderson was born in 1964. He has been through many incarnations including accountant, builder and cabinet maker, and at 58 has now discovered poetry.

*Unstructured* is his first collection of poems.

To my wife, Julie. She won't read it but she's very supportive.

Terrance Anderson

# UNSTRUCTURED

AUSTIN MACAULEY PUBLISHERS™
LONDON • CAMBRIDGE • NEW YORK • SHARJAH

Copyright © Terrance Anderson 2024

The right of Terrance Anderson to be identified as author of this work has been asserted by the author in accordance with sections 77 and 78 of the Copyright, Designs and Patents Act 1988.

All rights reserved. No part of this publication may be reproduced, stored in a retrieval system, or transmitted in any form or by any means, electronic, mechanical, photocopying, recording, or otherwise, without the prior permission of the publishers.

Any person who commits any unauthorised act in relation to this publication may be liable to criminal prosecution and civil claims for damages.

A CIP catalogue record for this title is available from the British Library.

ISBN 9781035815586 (Paperback)
ISBN 9781035815593 (ePub e-book)

www.austinmacauley.com

First Published 2024
Austin Macauley Publishers Ltd®
1 Canada Square
Canary Wharf
London
E14 5AA

# Lyme Sunrise

5 am and Lyme is bliss,
There's rarely a time when Lyme's as peaceful as this.
No people, no dogs, just the gulls and me,
A gentle breeze and the barely perceptible swish of the sea.
The sun not up but the sky is now bright,
Boats bob by the cobb as I wait for the sun to shoo off the night.
The sun rising now – a beautiful ball,
A glow in the sky, crimson streak on the water, and just me to witness it all.
Then I wander the front, then I wander the streets,
Just me and the gulls and the gentle tattoo of my feet.
But now I'll be off and get myself home,
And remember this place, and the peace, and the time that I sat and I watched the sun rise here alone.

# Beauty

Time has not withered thy beauty, for beauty such as thine
Runs too deep for those hands to reach.
Indeed, Old Father must needs join with an army
Of woes to turn such beauty sour.

# 31 Years

I wanted to write a poem, but as I try the words won't come
To tell you how I feel after all these years...
To say that you don't look a mess if your hair needs a little TLC...
To say that even if you think there is a little more of you, I just see it as a little more to hold...
To say that 31 years is not enough...
I wanted to write a poem but it just sounded trite,
I wanted to but it means too much!
And all I want to tell you is, despite what the song says, there is no room in my heart because it's full of you!

# Anger

There is an anger inside me I have no right to lay claim to.

What put it there I cannot say, for I have no trauma in my history to justify this thing that mauls me from within.

No misuse, no grief on which to hang a date. And yet it is there – lurking below the surface – waiting to explode.

Most days, thankfully, it lays so low you would not know, yet some it boils and ferments and wants to shout, smash, rage, tear the world to pieces.

Those are the days I have to stop, breathe deep, think of beaches, take a step back.

I push it away and refuse it entry, "No!" I say, "you cannot enter here."

I know if I succumb, I will regret.

I will hate the hate.

I will be angry at the anger for taking my place.

I will cry and say sorry.

But the worm of regret will gnaw away with its toothless gums.

This anger inside me should not be there, and yet must never get out.

# Borders

Oh, to do away with borders and the trouble they bring.
To rid ourselves of the saber rattling hatred from one side to the other.
To stop the alpha male grandstanding.
The showmanship and brinkmanship.
The greed.
The power hunger.
The need to dominate and control.
Oh, to be able to step from one place to another without scrutiny.
To see each other as other people not as bloody foreigners.
Imagine a true global community.
A single planet, not a hoard of countries and a spider's web of boundaries.
Oh, to sit and listen to peace…not to fear the thunder of war.

# Dad – The Visit

I visit, we talk, but not very much.
Mostly you sleep and wake with a confusion it's hard to comprehend.
"Have you sorted it out yet?"
"Sorted what Dad?"
"That…mmm…you were working on," pointing vaguely across the room.
"It's fine Dad, it's all sorted," though I have no idea what I've heroically mended this time.
The football's on. "I just don't understand it anymore, they kick the ball around and then cuddle a lot."
I make sympathetic noises.
I feel it should be worrying or frightening, or something but you just seem to take your total inability to understand life in your stride.


I can't understand, I can't explain it, I don't know when I last saw that person.
But never mind, that's just the way it is.
I guess all that knowledge is still in there somewhere, but the connections have been blocked. Some permanently, some coming back now and then.
If I start a quote you finish it without hesitation, better than I can, and yet you have no idea who made your breakfast.

With the TV blaring you fall once again to sleep, dreams soon to be confused with reality. Sleeping your way slowly to the great unknown.

Are you sad?
Are you happy?
Are you simply drifting onward?

No, there is frustration sometimes. Garbled explanations, words that won't behave, then "what the hell happened?"
But fortunately it passes, you move on, you sleep.
I miss you, Dad!

# Discontent

Sometimes I feel fucked up inside.
Discontent and resentment beating at the walls of my soul,
Not the person I was meant to be.
I think of school and how different it could have been, should have been…
A little more effort,
A plea for help,
Not just written off as thick because I wasn't academic.
A request from a teacher to send me to choir school quashed by my parents.
I hear a voice in song and feel my throat try to emulate the sound.
I hear music and get lost in the rhythm and emotion,
I see familiar faces on screen and long to recite another's words.
Become – for a time – another person
Transform myself while others look on…
I yearn to lose myself in the life and character and feelings of another,
Then I look at myself and what I am and fight off the bitterness of what could have been …
I am what I am!
I have what I have!
But sometimes it just feels wrong.

# Envy

What beast is this that sits heavy on my shoulder and bends my mind to crave such words as could come from another's pen?

Why can I not be content with those thoughts that come natural to mine own creation but must seek to emulate the genius of another?

Oh, to be able to steal the mood of any man and replace it with another as the whim takes me.

To wet the eye of a woman for whom the sun until now hath lit her day.

To take a man with spirits so low as to commune with the beetles and worms, then lift them to frolic as cows set loose after a winter's incarceration.

But alas! Such skill is beyond my hand and never will such poetry be put to paper from my pen.

I doff my hat to the Bard.

# Friends

I love to be with friends—
The quiet, comfortable banter,
The easy sharing of a glass or two,
Discussions that almost, but not quite, turn to arguments—
Knowing you can never truly offend them…
The warmth that comes from knowing they are there for you
And you for them,
The feeling that however long you are apart you will just take up where you left off.
The happiness of knowing you are 'one of us'
Friends!

# Greener Grass

This is not my life as it should be
I meet you after so long and I think, 'I wish I'd done what you did'
I think how interesting your work is—
Not humdrum,
Not run-of-the-mill at all,
I imagine a life a little more affluent…
I see enjoyment of the finer side of life…
A little more wine—
Restaurants perhaps
Visits to foreign climbs,
We talk about our lives and what we've seen
The journeys we've been on,
Our families and our friends—
Even the films we like to watch
But then you tell me,
'I wish I'd done what you did'

# In the Garden

To sit of a summer's eve next to a fire in my garden, and drink in the sounds and smells that warm days leave us to enjoy.
Such peace.
Leaning back and gazing into the sky, I watch the extraordinary god-fight played out by the swifts.
No shots fired.
No casualties sustained.
Swooping and diving, chasing at breakneck speed, avoiding collisions with a deftness that defies belief.
Peep, peep peeping as they career through the gloom in search of tiny morsels to eat.
Entranced, I watch their balletic performance for a time slowed down, until suddenly they are gone, leaving me to the ebb and flow of the embered foundations of my fire.
I listen as it crackles, I watch flames entangle and part, reaching for heights forever beyond their grasp.
Slowly the fire dies to intricate, throbbing, glowing ghosts
Mere memories of the wood I put on.
Soon the heat goes, and so do I…

# Insomnia

Mind racing
Thoughts rushing
Excitement boiling
Can't sleep

# Inspiration

I have no inspiration, yet I feel the urge to write.
I haven't taken long, lazy walks beneath boughs or cloudless skies.
I haven't listened to wind and wave crashing against rocks along the shore.
I haven't sat and supped with friends, laughing, talking, arguing into the night.
I spend my days toiling over wood to make furniture for folk so much wealthier than I, but no inspiration comes from there.
And yet I feel the need to put pen to paper, one word after another.
Perhaps, soon, inspiration will come…

# Jubilee

The bunting and scarecrows can all go away,
The party food and bottles of beer served their purpose for the day
The celebrations over, frivolity all done,
We played the games, we had a laugh, we chatted in the sun.
The children had a whale, the adults all got drunk,
Some quite as royally as a pie-eyed skunk.
I had a go at welly wanging, but couldn't wang it very far,
Maybe I'd spent a little too long standing at the bar.
We toasted the queen and her 70 years,
Yes, we all raised our glasses and gave her three cheers.
Prizes were given for scarecrows and cakes,
Then we all got to sample some very fine bakes.
But the party soon ended and we wandered away,
But we'll remember it fondly, that splendid day.

# Little Compass

I love my little compass
It's only very small,
But I've had my little compass
Since I wasn't very tall,
I've done a bit of traveling
Not exactly far and wide,
But I've always had my little compass
Right there by my side,
It shows me where the North is the
South, the West and East,
And in my little compass
I have a friend with me at least.

# Monday Morning

Long faces
Subdued, happy greetings
Slow moves towards the bench
Lunches into the fridge
Teas and coffees made
Talk of the weekend's doings
Feet dragged towards the inevitable 7am
Heads down
Conversations continue
Another Monday morning

# Regret and Rebirth

Spreadeagled on the lawn
As naked as the dawn
This is no kind of porn
Just my self-respect torn
I watch the stars adorn
The sky before the morn
Cold, wet, forlorn
It is my happiness I mourn
For the anger and the scorn
With which I left all lovers shorn

But in the dew, I feel reborn
Like a prancing little fawn
My demeanor now respawned
I shall not leave love lorn
No longer feeling tired and worn
To convention, I'll conform
Now that I am newly formed
Spreadeagled on the lawn

# Remember

The shelling has stopped.
There are no cries anymore.
Death hangs not in a barbed-wire fence, nor half submerged in a waterlogged crater.
Today the sun shines down, unobscured by smoke or gas.
Peace reigns.
You are many, calm now, not frightened.
At rest.
We took our shilling, did our duty.
Suffered the nights, endured the days.
We envied the rats that could scurry away.
Hell crept over this earth for a time.
Dark, dismal, noisy, smelly, shell-shocked hell.
A hell of mud, flies, decay, cries in the night, and fear.
But it's over now.
And to those of you who we left behind, know that we took you with us.

# River

Ebullient, turbulent, chaotic.
These words I could use to describe your progress, or peaceful, enchanting, relaxing.
Rolling, quietly bubbling, caressing the rocks as you follow your persistent path to the sea.
Emerging slowly from the grandeur of the Exmoor heights, gathering pace, fed from every angle, giving life in all directions.
Rushing, spilling, never stopping, chattering as you go, like whispered voices, perhaps the ghosts of the Doons plotting still.
But plots will come to nought as you carry their secrets to the channel, your wider travels to begin.

# Secret Thoughts

Secret thoughts, private dreams
Things are not always what they are
One thing may be as one appearance but aspire to another all the while
A mouse roaring like a lion
Form and desire not in sync
A burden that must be born, or a decision to be made?
Hiding in the shadows beneath the rough, or legitimise the adornment of softer things?
But change takes change beyond the change
Kicking against the norm
Bravery enough to match the need
But for some time and circumstance conspire against the nod
Where lives entwine, emotions confuse
Too much to lose
Too much heartache to cause
A secret it is then, close to the heart
No transformation
Love the loved
Live as lived
Never utter a word

# Sleep Father, Sleep

Sleep Father, sleep. Rest your mind for in truth there is precious little left.

The intellect that once would regale, amuse and teach us must surely still live on but the connection with the outside world seems lost or broken.

Broken beyond repair though occasional flashes of the old shine through.

There is no anger, no rages at what you have become, just a quiet, content acceptance.

Sleep Father, sleep. Against a backdrop of booming television, waking at times unable to distinguish dreams from reality.

Telling of your trip to the Himalayas with Micheal, so sure you can leave your chair whenever you want.

Sleep Father, sleep. And when you wake to find that I have gone, leaving you to your adventures, will you notice my empty seat?

Will you know that, once again, you are alone, gazing at the television, unfolding scene after scene incomprehensibly before you? Waiting, unaware, for your next meal to be served.

Sleep Father, sleep. Sleep away your allotment, but fret not and know this of us, that we love you and miss you, and will miss you harder when the sleeper wakes no more.

# Strength

Gently swaying to and fro, breeze pushed twigs,
Branches join the dance as a soft wind lifts the beat
The heavier the wind the more troubled the wood
Pushed and shoved,
Bent and twisted,
Fibers strained,
Movement adding strength
Strength gained from adversity
Yet not always
Oftentimes adversity saps such strength as was and leaves a shell
A broken husk,
A sad outline,
No strength from adversity, just adversity from strength

# The Calm After the Storm

Inactivity born of necessity
Creation of sensitivity,
Then cool efficiency takes over, calming the inner panic
Jocularity and banter belie the quiet confidence
All the time chatting,
Chatting,
Chatting…

All the time efficient
Breathe deeply
Then in an instant, all has changed!
A different ceiling, more jokes, more efficiency

Not quiet though, not peaceful
Noise all around
Alarm going off
Equipment clanging
People talking, sometimes shouting
But still a night's sleep
A quick check
Then home.

# The Darkness

There is a darkness that descends upon me, creeping like a malevolent force into my brain.
On bright days or gloomy the smallest of things can invite the beast in.
This cloud
This hole
This dissenting voice making me question my worth. Making me question if I'm capable of…what?
Anything and everything.
Would I be missed if suddenly I were gone?
But yes, I think perhaps I would.
Me? I am fortunate.
I can shake the darkness, unlike so many other poor souls.
Until next time…

# The Pool

We hear the screams long before we reach the scene.
Loud noise. People shouting.
Then we see the glint of water over the fence.
At any other time the screams could be a portent of some horror to come, the shouts perhaps fear or defiance.
Not here.
Not today.
As we glimpse the water I feel elated. It is a cool invitation, a summons, a call to joy.
I can't wait to join the noise as we enter the pool, ready to vocalise our own excitement.
I plunge in and all is silent for a few seconds until I emerge once more into the melee.
What next?
Make a decision.
The rapids.
We wait our turn then down we go.
Tumbling, turning we submerge and surface, laughter bringing us together.
Next a flume.
The adrenaline from the speed, the moment of panic as I drop backwards into the void.
But the void is not a void, it scoops us up and spins us round and spews us out to the final mad splash at the bottom.
Then rapids.

Then slides and flumes and round and round until we finally stop, bruised, exhausted and laughing.

Dry and clothed again we wander off, the screams the last thing we hear of the pool.

# True Friends

We should all have friends
Not the transient e-friends on this week's favourite platform
Not the huggy-kissy, lovey-dovey kind that last as long as fashion
Not the sofa crashing, sponging, self-absorbed kind
But the real kind…
The 'call me if you need me day or night' kind,
The ones you could not see for 6 months but it feels like 6 minutes,
The kind who will do what they can to help you out,
The 'look you up after 40 years' because they can – kind
True friends!

# When I Am Gone

What will they think of me when I am gone?
How will they remember the way I have lived?
Will people think fondly or praise the day I slipped away?
Should I even care?
This mortal anxiety is but a shallow fear and when sleep returns us not to consciousness,
what matter the legacy we leave behind?
If skeletons skulk within my cupboards, I won't know if they suddenly appear.

But when all's said and done really what does it matter?
If the reputation built up is summarily shattered,
If my good name is taken and beaten and battered,
If the threads carefully laid to the 4 winds are scattered,

But I know of no misdeeds to chase me to the grave.
No secrets to be unmasked to shock those left behind.
And in the end, I still hope that remembrance will be fond.

# Worries

Trials and worries shake and topple spirits
Necessities beyond the means
Time too pressing to lighten the load
Succour offered seems sadly inadequate
9 to 5 an endless drudge of frustration and tedium
Feeling the world is turning to shit
Dark clouds tug at our sleeves at times of adversity
Boredom dragging us down.
But where is the line that legitimises these feelings?
Is there a selfishness of scale?
So many worse off
Or is comparison an acceptable leveller?
Your life mangled by war
My cosy existence shaken by a lesser struggle
Minor to you, great to me.
Where is the line?

Made in the USA
Monee, IL
03 May 2026